# *Entertaining with Amy*

*by Amy Lawrence*

Published by:
ATR Publishing

Photos by:
Patrick Lawrence and Rachael Grafe Travis

Back Cover Photo by:
Sirlin Photographers
(916)444-8464
http://www.sirlin.com/

Copyright © 2012 ATR Publishing

All rights reserved. No part of this publication may be reproduced in any form or by any means, electronic or mechanical, including photocopy and information storage and retrieval system, without permission in writing from the author.

## *Dedication*

I would like to dedicate "Entertaining with Amy" to my husband and children. They have all been instrumental in creating this cookbook. They have been great taste testers. They put up with eating the same food many days in a row while I perfect the "right" version of the recipe. My son, Thomas, has done countless amounts of dirty dishes during this whole process. Jacob, has been a great inspiration for new ideas. Pat, the love of my life, has done everything from creating a computer program (to lay out the book design), to editing, to taking pictures and even washing dishes. Without him, this book would have not been written.

I would like to thank the following people: Rachel Grafe Travis, my Pilates instructor, for helping me with the cover photo (as well as not scolding me as to why I wasn't making progress on my weight goal while writing and testing recipes for this book), Col. Thomas and Barb Culling, Stan and Michele Lawrence, Amy Nelson, Babette Donaldson, Monique Juarez, Julie Carlin and Wendy Bryant for inspiration and support. I would also like to thank my customers. You all have supported me over the years by buying my teas and cookbooks. Without you, none of this would be possible. Thank you!

Last but not least, I would like to thank my grandmother, Alice McCoy where my passion for cookbook writing began. She instilled in me the love of cooking and good food. When she passed away in 2004, she left me money which I used to

## *Dedication Continued*

print my first cookbook, "Creating an Afternoon to Remember".

*"My mom and I have tea every morning and she makes us great dinners every night. She is without a doubt the best cook I know and I am so fortunate to have her."*
    – Thomas Patton, 16

*"My mom is the best cook I know and her food has been one of the largest experiences of my life. I remember when she taught me how to make how to make eggs. My favorite thing is parties. My mom has a cookbook party once a year and they are the best with lots of delicious food. I don't think my life would be the same without 'An Afternoon to Remember'."*
    – Jacob Lawrence, 12

# *Foreword*

As many of you know, I love to entertain my family and friends. One of my favorite things to do in life is to spend the day cooking in preparation for a big party at my house. Making people happy with my food brings me joy as do all of the great leftovers! For my parties I like to go all out and make everything taste as fresh and good as it possibly can be. My advice to you is to use only quality ingredients. Don't skimp.

Most of these recipes are meant to be dishes you make for friends and family. Some of them are calorie laden so you might not want them for "every day" dishes but rather save them for a special occasion (Jamaican Banana Cheesecake – page 135). Some take a bit of time but they are well worth it, especially if you freeze them (Amy's Suiza Con Pollo Enchiladas – page 67). Spending hours on dishes that barely make enough or lack in taste is a waste of time, resources, and energy. I feel if it's going to take some time, then it should be absolutely wonderful and provide lots of leftovers.

It's always amazing to me, how many people do not actually "cook" at all these days. Obviously this isn't you or you wouldn't have purchased this cookbook. With our busy schedules some people find that it's often easier to serve something already prepared and sometimes that's true and necessary. However, there are also ways to make home cooking convenient for you (such as making a big batches, freezing leftovers, etc). I like knowing what ingredients are in my meals. When you take the time to make it yourself, the results

## *Foreword Continued*

make it worthwhile. The foods taste better and almost always it is better for you.

Many of the recipes in this book are meant to go together. By preparing compatible foods your valuable time is more wisely spent when the recipe can used for other dishes. For example, if you make Ginger Scallion Sauce (page 59), it will keep up to a week. It can be used in the Sichuan Chicken Flatbread (page 103) and in the Ginger Scallion Salmon (page 95). Add it to scrambled eggs or toss a few tablespoons in a salad for an extra treat. Make it once and use it for many dishes. In this way your family doesn't get tired of the same leftovers and you can have great dishes without starting from scratch. Feel free to mix and match recipes. The Spicy Dragon Sauce (page 63) was originally meant to go with the Sichuan Chicken Flatbread, but my son, Jacob, told me one day, "Mom, the chicken filling would be great in an egg roll." He was so right! Thanks to his taste buds we've added the Spicy Dragon Sauce to the Sichuan Chicken Flatbread, the Chicken Sichuan Egg Rolls (page 23), and the Asparagus and Ham Roll Ups (page 19). These options are a great reward for the time and effort you spent to make the recipe. The same thing goes for the Tomatillo Green Salsa (page 51). It's great with chips, as a salad dressing and in tacos. Add one more ingredient and it suddenly turns into Chipotle Salsa or use it in Amy's Suiza Con Pollo Enchiladas.

It is my sincere hope that you use and enjoy this book. I've

## *Foreword Continued*

had lots of fun creating it.

Happy Cooking!

With much love,

Amy

# Table of Contents

## Appetizers

| | |
|---|---|
| Amarula Brown Sugar Pecan Brie | 15 |
| Asparagus and Ham Roll Ups | 19 |
| Cajun French Bread | 21 |
| Chicken Sichuan Egg Rolls | 23 |
| Chinese Scallion Pancakes | 27 |
| Chipotle Salsa | 31 |
| Fresh Tomato and Mozzarella Kabobs | 33 |
| Homemade Corn Tortillas | 35 |
| Homemade Salami Made with Lapsang Souchong Tea | 37 |
| Rosemary Garlic Parmesan Pinwheels | 41 |
| Savory Ham and Cheddar Scones | 45 |
| Sundried Tomato Dip | 49 |
| Tomatillo Green Salsa | 51 |

## Seasonings & Sauces

| | |
|---|---|
| Amy's Homemade Taco Seasoning | 57 |
| Ginger Scallion Sauce | 59 |
| Spicy Dragon Sauce | 63 |

## Main Dishes, Sides & Salads

| | |
|---|---|
| Amy's Suiza Con Pollo Enchiladas | 67 |
| Cantaloup Caprese Salad | 71 |
| Caprese Salad | 73 |
| Cilantro Pork Crock Pot | 77 |

# Table of Contents Continued

## Main Dishes, Sides & Salads

| | |
|---|---|
| Delicious Healthy Breakfast Burrito | 79 |
| Easy 40 Clove Garlic Crock Pot Chicken | 83 |
| Easy Open Faced Chicken and Asparagus Sandwich Melts | 87 |
| Käse Spätzle | 89 |
| Pat's Sliders | 93 |
| Ginger Scallion Salmon | 95 |
| Sesame Chicken | 97 |
| Sichuan Chicken Flatbread | 103 |
| Street Tacos | 107 |
| Wiener Schnitzel | 111 |

## Desserts

| | |
|---|---|
| Buttered Rum Sauce Mix | 117 |
| Apple Cake with Buttered Rum Sauce | 119 |
| Caramel Choc Bars | 121 |
| Easy Raspberry Lime Tarts | 127 |
| Easy Sea Salt Toffee Candy | 131 |
| Jamaican Banana Cheesecake | 135 |
| Oodles (Oatmeal Snickerdoodles) | 141 |
| Orange Walnut Scones | 145 |
| Peppermint Brittle | 149 |

## Drinks

| | |
|---|---|
| Ginger Syrup | 155 |

## *Table of Contents Continued*

### Drinks

| | |
|---|---|
| Pat's Ecotinis | 157 |
| Peach Bowle | 159 |

*Appetizers*

## *Amarula Brown Sugar Pecan Brie*

My friend, Amy Nelson, brought this to a party, but she made it with Kahlua. I thought it might work well with Amarula which is a cream liqueur from South Africa that we discovered on our cruise to the Mexican Riviera. It definitely does and is absolutely delicious, not to mention easy!

- 1 wheel of brie (the 19 oz. one from Costco works great)
- 1 c. Amarula cream liqueur
- 1 c. light brown sugar, packed
- 1 c. toasted pecans (I like to leave them whole because I think they look prettier that way, but you can chop them if you want.)

Preheat oven to 350°. Place pecans on a cookie sheet and toast for about 5 minutes. Set aside. Carefully slice the top off of the Brie wheel, but do not remove completely. Bake for

*Notes*

## *Amarula Brown Sugar Pecan Brie Continued*

15 minutes at 350°. Remove the top of the brie.

In a medium sauce pan while the brie is baking, bring Amarula and brown sugar to a boil and simmer for 10-15 minutes. Add the toasted pecans and simmer for another few minutes. Pour the mixture over the brie and serve with crackers.

*Notes*

## *Asparagus Ham Roll Ups*

I just love the Spicy Dragon Sauce so I came up with an easy appetizer that you can dip into that delicious sauce!

- ½ lb. deli ham, sliced very thin
- 1 bunch of asparagus
- Spicy Dragon Sauce (page 63)

Trim off the ends of asparagus spears. Cook asparagus until just tender. I usually cook mine for a few minutes in the microwave wrapped in a damp paper towel. Rinse with cold water. Pat dry.

Place a piece of ham on a cutting board. Place an asparagus spear at one end and roll up tightly (like a rug). Cut roll into small pieces. Secure each roll with a toothpick. Place on appetizer tray and serve with Spicy Dragon Sauce.

*Notes*

# Cajun French Bread

This is a twist on traditional garlic bread. Make it as spicy as you want!

- 1 loaf of French bread
- ¼ c. butter, melted
- Cajun seasoning
- 2 cloves garlic, minced
- ¼ t. cayenne pepper
- 1 t. rosemary
- ½ c. Parmesan cheese, shredded

Slice French bread into two halves. Melt butter in a small bowl in the microwave. Stir in garlic, cayenne, and rosemary. Spread on each half of French bread. Top with parmesan cheese. Sprinkle each half with Cajun seasoning. Bake or broil until cheese is melted. Cut into slices.

Makes 1 loaf of Cajun French Bread.

*Notes*

## Chicken Sichuan Egg Rolls

These take a bit of time to make, but they are oh so delicious! The great thing about them is they freeze well. Store them in the freezer and fry up when you have a craving. I like to have an "Egg Roll Party" where we make a double batch then invite friends over to help roll, fry and eat.

- 2 chicken breasts, cut in small pieces
- ½ c. red cabbage, finely chopped
- 1 clove of garlic, minced
- 1 T. sesame oil
- 1 T. Ginger Scallion Sauce (page 59) or use 6 green onions chopped
- 3 green onions, chopped
- salt and pepper to taste
- 2 c. shredded Monterey Jack – Pepper Jack also works well
- 1 pkg. won ton wrappers (about 40-50 in a package)

*Notes*

## *Chicken Sichuan Egg Rolls Continued*

- 1 egg

Heat sesame oil in a medium skillet, add chopped chicken and cook until done. Drain chicken and return to pan. Add garlic, cabbage, ginger scallion sauce or green onions. Add salt and pepper to taste. Add shredded cheese and cook on low just until cheese is melted. Turn off heat.

Beat eggs in a small bowl. Take egg roll wrappers out of package and place on a large cutting board. Place a damp paper towel over wrappers while you work.

Place a wrapper on the cutting board, with a point side toward you. Spoon about ½ T. of meat mixture into the center of the wrapper. Dip finger into egg and spread it onto opposite triangle of wrapper. Roll up egg roll about half-way and pull in edges, continue rolling and seal outside of point with more beaten egg. Place on a cookie sheet lined with parchment paper. Place a damp paper towel over the top so the egg rolls do not dry out. Refrigerate until you are ready to fry them (do not leave in refrigerator more than 1 day). Although I think they are best the same day, you can also freeze them. Flash freeze them on the cookie sheet and then transfer to a ziplock bag. When you're ready to cook them, thaw them out slightly before frying.

To fry:

Heat deep fryer or oil in a pan on stove to about 375°. Deep fry until golden brown. Drain on paper towels.

Serve with Spicy Dragon Sauce (page 63) or soy sauce.

Makes about 40-50 egg rolls.

*Notes*

## *Chinese Scallion Pancakes*

These are great to eat alone or use them to make Sichuan Chicken Flatbread (page 103). There are many different ways to make scallion pancakes. Some people roll and layer each pancake separately but I think this way is the easiest. They store very well in the refrigerator up to a week.

- 2 c. flour
- ¾ c. boiling water
- 2 bunches of green onions, finely chopped
- 2 T. sesame seeds
- Sesame oil
- Sea salt

Place flour in food processor. Slowly add boiling water and pulse until mixture forms a ball. Cover with a damp cloth and allow dough to sit at least 10 minutes before rolling into

*Notes*

## *Chinese Scallion Pancakes Continued*

pancakes.

When ready to make the pancakes, roll dough out on a floured board into a large rectangle as thin as you can. Use a pastry brush or spoon to spread a thin layer of sesame oil evenly over dough. Sprinkle with sesame seeds, green onions and salt. Roll the dough up like a rug. Cut or break off dough into 8 pieces. Take each piece and twist, like you are wringing a dish rag. Then flatten and roll into a pancake as thin as you can get it. Do this for all 8 pancakes. Place in between well-oiled wax paper or parchment paper as you finish rolling out each one. At this point you can cook them on a griddle using the directions below or store them in between the waxed or parchment papers in a plastic bag for up to 1 week. Makes 8 pancakes.

When ready to cook, heat a tablespoon of oil on a griddle or flat pan skillet on medium high heat. Place the pancake in the oil and let fry until the bottom is crisp. Flip over pancake and cook until done. Add more oil as needed when frying the pancakes. Serve immediately or reheat in the oven.

If serving them alone as pancakes, sprinkle extra salt over the top after frying. If using them for Sichuan Flat Bread, do not add extra salt.

*Notes*

## *Chipotle Salsa*

I created a spicer version of the Tomatillo Green Salsa by adding Chipotle peppers to my already great tomatillo salsa. My family likes this one even better. When I'm having a party, I make the Tomatillo Green Salsa and reserve part of it for this one. That way I have a mild green salsa and a spicy red salsa. They have totally different tastes so try making both of them!

- 2 c. Tomatillo Green Salsa (page 51)
- 1 can of Chipotle peppers in Adobo sauce

Take out 4 of the peppers from the Chipotle can. Process in a food processor. Add to 2 c. of the Tomatillo Green Salsa. Enjoy!

To make it more spicy – add another pepper, less spicy – one less pepper.

*Notes*

## *Fresh Tomato and Mozzarella Kabobs*

My neighbor, Brenda, brought these to a party and I thought they were fantastic. It's a great way to add something fresh and light to a heavy appetizer menu. Serve with a good balsamic vinegar or Italian dressing if desired.

- grape tomatoes or small cherry tomatoes
- mozarella pearls or mozarella slices cut into cubes
- fresh basil
- freshly cracked pepper
- balsamic vinegar – use a good quality one, my favorite brand comes from Monterey called, "Coeur D'Olives". They have a black currant balsamic vinegar that's absolutely divine! You can find it on www.afternoontoremember.com
- cocktail toothpicks, the longer the better

Throughly wash tomatoes and basil and pat dry. Skewer tomato, basil leaf, and mozzarella. Serve with balsamic vinegar or Italian dressing.

*Notes*

## *Homemade Corn Tortillas*

This recipe isn't mine but it's on the back of the Masa Harina. I put it in the cookbook because many people do not realize how easy it is to make tortillas and I also wanted to give you some tips on making them. I make mine small because I like using them for appetizers.

- 2 c. Masa - Instant Corn Masa Flour (loosely measured, not packed, I buy Maseca brand)
- ¼ t. salt
- 1¼ c. water

Mix Masa and salt together. Add water and stir for a few minutes until mixture comes to a ball. If dough feels dry, add more water, 1 tablespoon at a time. Divide into 16 balls. Place between two sheets of parchment paper. Use a glass pie plate as a press or a tortilla press. Press down on ball of dough until a nice circle is formed. Carefully peel off parchment paper and transfer to a hot ungreased griddle or frying pan. You do not need to add oil or spray to the pan. Cook for about 1 minute on each side. Serve warm. This recipes makes about 16 small tortillas.

After they are cooked, you can store them in the refrigerator and then reheat them as needed. You can also fry them in oil for tostadas.

One note: Do not refrigerate masa dough before rolling or pressing them out or the dough will become too cold and break when you try to lift it off of the paper.

*Notes*

# *Homemade Salami Made with Lapsang Souchong Tea*

People are always surprised when I tell them that I made homemade salami. I get rave reviews, especially from men. This recipe is very easy and only has to sit 24 hours in the refrigerator before you can bake it. When I make it, I usually make a triple batch using 6 lbs. of hamburger. It's the perfect appetizer to take to parties. You can also store it in the freezer and give it away as gifts during the holidays.

- 2 lbs. ground beef
- ¾ c. strongly brewed Lapsang Souchong tea (Make a strong cup using 2 T. tea in ¾ c. boiling water. Steep 5 min. 1 oz. pkg. of tea is plenty will make almost 3 batches)
- 1 t. granulated garlic. or garlic powder
- 1 t. dried onion
- 1 T. mustard seed

*Notes*

## *Homemade Salami Made with Lapsang Souchong Tea Continued*

- 2 T. Morton Tender Quick (you can find this in the salt section of specialty grocery stores, or order it on-line from Morton's)
- 2 t. liquid smoke flavoring
- 1 T. black pepper

In a large bowl, mix together the beef and tea. Add remaining ingredients. Mix very well with your hands. Form the mixture into 2 long logs and wrap with foil. Refrigerate for 24 hours. Preheat the oven to 350°. Remove the foil from the beef. Make a few slits in the bottom of the logs so the grease will drain while cooking. Place logs on a roasting rack in a shallow pan to catch the drippings. Bake for 1 hour. Cool, then wrap in plastic or foil and refrigerate. Makes 2 long logs. You can also smoke the salami on the grill using indirect heat. Grill it for 3 hours at 150°, then turn up temperature to about 225° and cook about 1 more hour or until salami reaches 155°.

Spicy Variation: Before baking roll the logs in black pepper. This spicy version is very popular so I usually roll 1 log in pepper and leave 1 plain.

*Notes*

# *Rosemary Garlic Parmesan Pinwheels*

There are many versions of pinwheels made with puff pastry. My version is a bit different. I love the buttery crispy taste of the parmesan cheese on top. For appetizers, I like to roll mine with the longest side toward you. It makes a smaller pinwheel but a great bite-sized appetizer. If you roll them the other way, you will have bigger pinwheels. You will have to bake it longer and it won't make as many. You can make these appetizers weeks ahead and have them ready in no time for unexpected guests.

- 1 pkg. frozen puff pastry sheets (17.3 oz.)
- ½ c. butter, melted
- 2 garlic cloves, minced
- 1 T. fresh rosemary, finely chopped
- ¼ t. cayenne
- 1 c. parmesan cheese, shredded

*Notes*

## *Rosemary Garlic Parmesan Pinwheels Continued*

- salt and pepper to taste

Take puff pastry out of the freezer and allow them to sit out for about 40 minutes. Do not thaw them much longer as it will be hard to work with the pastry.

In a small dish, melt the butter in the microwave. Add the minced garlic, rosemary and cayenne pepper. On a lightly floured surface, roll out one piece of puff pastry slightly with a rolling pin. You don't need to make it super thin, but just a bit thinner. Brush the puff pastry sheet with butter mixture. Sprinkle puff pastry sheet with salt, pepper and a bit of parmesan cheese. Starting with the longest side closest to you, roll up in jelly roll fashion (like a rug). Wrap in parchment paper and again in cellophane. Roll out the second puff pastry sheet and repeat the same procedure. Save the left-over butter mixture for later. Freeze rolls for about 1 hour (or longer if you are making them for a later use).

Preheat oven to 400°. Cut each roll into 40 slices. Lay out slices about 2 inches apart on a cookie sheet lined with parchment paper or foil (you need something as the cheese will stick to the surface). Brush each slice with the reserved butter mixture and top with grated parmesan cheese. Bake for about 7-14 minutes or until lightly browned. Serve warm or at room temperature.

The great thing about this appetizer is that you can make them weeks ahead of time. Just thaw a bit, slice, butter, sprinkle, bake and serve!

*Notes*

## *Savory Ham and Cheddar Scones*

These are perfect as a savory morning treat or with a nice salad. They also make great appetizers!

- 3 c. self-rising flour
- ⅛ c. sugar
- 1 garlic clove, minced
- 1 t. pepper
- 1 T. fresh rosemary, finely chopped
- ½-¾ c. white cheddar cheese (living in Seattle, I like to use Beecher's Flagship)
- 1½ c. ham, chopped (I use a ham steak, chopped in cubes, but deli ham would also work well)
- ½ c. unsalted butter, cold (one stick)
- 1 c. buttermilk (you may need more or less)

*Notes*

## *Savory Ham and Cheddar Scones Continued*

Preheat oven to 400°. Combine flour, sugar, garlic, rosemary and pepper. Cut in butter until mixture is course and crumbly. Stir in cheese and ham. Add just enough buttermilk to make a soft dough. Scoop out about ⅓ of the dough and form a small disc about 8 inches in diameter and about ½ inch thick. Cut disc into 8 pie-shaped pieces. Do this for the remaining dough. Place on a cookie sheet lined with parchment paper and bake until done, about 8-12 minutes. Makes about 24 scones.

If you want to use them as appetizers, scoop out about 1 c. of the dough, form a disc and cut into 8 tiny pieces. Repeat with remaining dough. These scones take about 5-8 minutes to bake. This batch will make about 50 appetizer-size scones.

Note: Because of the ham, the remaining uneaten scones need to be refrigerated or put them in a plastic bag and store them in the freezer until ready to reheat and eat.

*Notes*

## Sundried Tomato Dip

This is an adaptation from one of my favorite tea sandwiches. It tastes best when you make it a few days early. You can store it for about 1 week in the refrigerator. It is a wonderful spread for toasted dark rye bread or crackers. I love to serve it during the holidays.

- 1½ c. sun-dried tomatoes, chopped finely
- ½ c. parmesan cheese, grated
- 3 cloves garlic, minced
- 1 t. olive oil
- ¼ c. fresh oregano, finely chopped
- 1 t. dried oregano
- 1 8 oz. pkg. cream cheese, softened
- ½ c. sour cream

Beat cream cheese until smooth. Add all ingredients. Mix until well blended. Serve with dark rye bread or crackers.

If made ahead and stored in refrigerator, allow the mixture to warm slightly to room temperature before serving. If mixture is too thick, add a bit of sour cream to make it more creamy and spreadable.

*Notes*

## *Tomatillo Green Salsa*

I love fresh salsa! This one is mild. If you want it spicy check out Chipotle Salsa (page 31) which uses this one as a base. It's great on salads too! Roasting the tomatillos, chilies and jalapeño definitely make a difference, so don't skip this step. This salsa also freezes well.

- 2 lbs. tomatillos
- 1 can green chilies
- 2-3 poblano peppers (these are mild)
- ¼-½ jalapeño (depending on how hot you like it)
- 2 garlic cloves, minced
- ½ c. onion
- ½ c. cilantro leaves, chopped
- 1 t. lime juice – fresh, use if you need to add a bit more tang to salsa

*Notes*

## *Tomatillo Green Salsa Continued*

- 1 t. sugar – only if needed, depends on sweetness of tomatillos
- salt and pepper to taste

Soak the tomatillos in water to help remove the husks. Cut tomatillos, jalapeño and chilies in half and place on a foil lined baking sheet. Broil until slightly blackened – about 8 minutes or so. Remove skins of chilies and jalapeño.

In a food processor, combine tomatillos, ¼-½ jalapeño, chilies, onion, cilantro, garlic and process until smooth. Add lime, sugar, salt and pepper to taste.

Refrigerate until needed. This is a great salsa with chips as well as a sauce for Amy's Suiza Con Pollo Enchiladas (page 67), or Cilantro Pork Crock Pot (page 77). When I make this salsa, I always take half of it and turn it into Chipotle Salsa.

*Notes*

# Seasonings & Sauces

## *Amy's Homemade Taco Seasoning*

This seasoning is so easy to make and very economical compared to taco seasoning packets you buy at the store. Try to buy the spices in bulk for extra savings (Winco and Costco are great places to shop for bulk spices). 2-3 tablespoons of this seasoning equals 1 commercial taco seasoning packet.

- 3 T. chili powder
- 1½ t. granulated garlic or garlic powder
- ¾ t. chopped dried onion or onion powder
- 1½ t. crushed red pepper flakes
- 1½ t. dried oregano
- 1½ t. smoked paprika
- 2 T. ground cumin
- 1 T. sea salt (do not substitute regular salt or it will be too salty)
- 1 T. black pepper
- 1 T. beef flavored bouillon (I buy the Knorr brand called, "Caldo Con Sabor de Res", it is powdered beef bouillon, sometimes found in the Hispanic section or soup stock section.)

Combine all ingredients and place in a spice jar or plastic bag. Use for seasoning tacos, dips, etc. Anywhere you would use the taco seasoning packets. 3 Tablespoons of this seasoning equals 1 taco seasoning packet.

Makes 3 oz.

*Notes*

# *Ginger Scallion Sauce*

This sauce is so versatile! Use it in Chicken Sichuan Egg Rolls (page 23) and Ginger Scallion Salmon (page 95). It can also be added to anything from scrambled eggs, to chicken, to veggies and it even makes a great salad dressing.

- 3 bunches of green onions (about 3 c. when chopped into 1 inch lengths)
- 2 oz. fresh ginger root (if you can't weigh it, the root will be about the size of the palm of your hand)
- 1 c. grapeseed oil (or peanut oil or corn oil, not canola)
- ½ T. salt (yes, a tablespoon)
- 1 clove fresh garlic, minced
- 1 t. sherry
- 1 t. soy sauce

Chop/pulse green onions in the food processor until they are

# Notes

## *Ginger Scallion Sauce Continued*

finely chopped (not pureed). Place them into a very large cooking pot. Peel and cut ginger root into about 1 inch pieces. Place them into the food processor and pulse until finely chopped. Add them to the cooking pot. Add salt and garlic.

In a separate pan, heat oil until hot and barely starts to smoke. Carefully pour hot oil into the cooking pot and stand back. The mixture will sizzle and bubble. Allow mixture to cool to room temperature. Add sherry and soy sauce.

Makes about 2 c. of sauce. Store in the refrigerator for up to one week.

*Notes*

## *Spicy Dragon Sauce*

Use this as a dipping sauce for Sichuan Flatbread (page 103), Chicken Sichuan Egg Rolls (page 23), Asparagus and Ham Roll Ups (page 19), drizzle a little over barbeque pizza or use as a spread on sandwiches for an extra kick!

- 1 c. mayonnaise or light mayonnaise
- 1-3 T. srirachi hot chili sauce (I like to use 3 T.)
- 8 green onions, cut into 1 inch lengths
- 5 garlic cloves, peeled
- ¼ t. horseradish

Place all ingredients in a food processor and process until onions are finely chopped. Keep in refrigerator up to 2 weeks.

*Notes*

# Main Dishes, Sides & Salads

# *Amy's Suiza Con Pollo Enchiladas*

When I was in college, one of my favorite dishes was Suiza Con Pollo from a Mexican restaurant called Carlos O'Kelly's. I have created my own version which includes using kale. I always try to incorporate kale into my dishes as it's very healthy for you and my kids don't realize they are eating a super food. You can also substitute fresh spinach. These enchiladas do take a bit of time, but well worth the effort and they freeze very well. Since the Tomatillo Green Salsa keeps for about a week, I like to make it up a day earlier and make the enchiladas on a different day.

- 5 chicken breasts – cooked, chopped/shredded
- ½ onion, finely chopped
- 1½ pounds cream cheese, softened
- 6 cloves garlic, minced
- 1 can green chilies (large can)

*Notes*

## *Amy's Suiza Con Pollo Enchiladas Continued*

- black olives (optional)
- 2 bunches green onions, chopped
- 3 large leaves of kale or chard, finely chopped
- Monterey Jack cheese, shredded (I like to use Pepper Jack cheese)
- ¾ c. Tomatillo Green Salsa (page 51)
- Tortillas (I like to use the uncooked ones from Costco and fry them up on a skillet, no need to use oil if you use a non-stick pan, just heat pan, cook tortillas, before filling enchiladas)

Cook chicken in a pan of boiling water for about 20 minutes or until done. Cut/shred chicken.

In a large mixing bowl, beat cream cheese until soft. Add garlic, onions, kale, and green chilies. Beat until smooth. Add chopped chicken.

Place about ½ c. tomatillo salsa in a 9"x13" baking dish. Place about ¼ c. chicken filling on a tortilla, top with a spoonful of green onion, top with shredded cheese. Roll and place seam side down in baking dish on top of salsa. Do this for all of the tortillas until no filling is left. This is a large recipe, so I usually get about 15 enchiladas. I make 2 pans and freeze one for later. After enchiladas are all filled, top with a little tomatillo salsa and sprinkle with more cheese. Cover with foil and bake in oven at 350° until heated thoroughly. Take foil off last 5 minutes or so of baking.

Makes about 15 enchiladas.

*Notes*

## *Cantaloup Caprese Salad*

Sometimes simple is best! One day I decided to try cantaloupe in my caprese salad. It was wonderful! To jazz it up a bit, I thought I might make a balsamic glaze instead of just balsamic vinegar. Then I thought, "Keep it simple". Sure enough it is delicious with just these ingredients. You can add olive oil, if you want, but I actually like mine without it. I thought it was such a unique salad, but apparently there are others out there. So much for being new!

- ½ cantaloupe, cut into bite-sized pieces (my trick for good tasting melons is to let them sit on counter to ripen for a few days before cutting)
- 2-3 tomatoes, very fresh and ripe
- Mozzarella – you can buy the mozzarella pearls or just cut up mozzarella balls into bite-sized pieces
- fresh basil leaves – the amount is up to you, for a single salad serving I use about 4 leaves
- balsamic vinegar – use a good quality one, my favorite brand comes from Monterey called, "Coeur D'Olives". They have a black currant balsamic vinegar that's absolutely divine! You can find it on www.afternoontoremember.com
- salt and pepper to taste

Mix cantaloupe, tomatoes, mozzarella and basil leaves. Season with salt and pepper according to taste. Drizzle balsamic vinegar all over. Enjoy!

*Notes*

## *Caprese Salad*

Living in California for almost 16 years, this salad became a staple at our house. Since tomatoes were so plentiful, we ate a version of this almost every evening during the summer with dinner. Fresh tomatoes are a must! Since it is so easy to put together, I didn't really think of it as a recipe until my family from Missouri and friends from Washington asked for the recipe. Here it is!

- fresh tomatoes, any kind, my favorites are roma and heirloom, chopped
- fresh basil leaves – the amount is up to you, for a single salad serving I use about 4 leaves, rinse leaves, stack together, roll and cut
- fresh mozzarella (optional) – you can buy the small mozzarella pearls or just cut up mozzarella balls into bite-sized pieces

*Notes*

## *Caprese Salad Continued*

- 2 t. red onion (optional), chopped
- 1 garlic clove, minced
- balsamic vinegar – use a good quality one, my favorite brand comes from Monterey called, "Coeur D'Olives". They have a black currant balsamic vinegar that's absolutely divine! You can find it on www.afternoontoremember.com
- olive oil (in Washington I like to buy Omega Evoo, my friend Nick Patlias' family owns the company and brings it over from Greece.)
- salt to taste
- fresh cracked black pepper to taste

Mix, tomatoes, basil, mozzarella, red onions and garlic. Season with salt and pepper according to taste. Drizzle balsamic vinegar over all. Enjoy! This salad tastes best if made up to 30 minutes before serving.

Although you can refrigerate the leftovers, I think it's best if eaten the same day. Some people like to cut the tomatoes into slices and then layer the tomatoes, basil and mozzarella. I prefer mine chopped into smaller pieces so I don't need a knife to eat the salad.

*Notes*

## *Easy Cilantro Crock Pot Pork*

I made this recipe up early one morning with ingredients I had on hand when I needed to be gone all day. It's been a favorite ever since! We eat it on rice, in tortillas, over nachos or on sandwiches. It's very versatile!

- 1 onion, chopped
- 6 porkchops, or 1 pork roast
- 2 cloves garlic, minced
- ½ jar of salsa (16 oz. jar) or 1 c. of Tomatillo Green Salsa (page 51)
- 2 cans of black beans
- 1 c. fresh cilantro

Put all ingredients in the crock pot. Cook on high for about 4 hours, or on low for 6-8 hours.

Serves 4-6.

*Notes*

# *Delicious Healthy Breakfast Burrito*

Many of you are already familiar with my Scrambled Eggs and Kale recipe from "Amy's Favorite Recipes", this is another version of it and is a great breakfast – a healthy way to start your day! It's very quick to make and you can easily vary the ingredients. I have since added all kinds of left-overs to the eggs, including cooked asparagus, zucchini, green beans, basically any vegetable I have in my refrigerator. I find that if I don't eat this for breakfast, I seem to be hungry all day. If you don't have any left-over vegetables, then cut up some fresh ones and microwave them for a few minutes before adding them to your skillet. You can find the uncooked tortillas in the refrigerator section of many grocery stores and also at Costco. They really are much better than the regular tortillas. The texture is amazing! Now that I've found these, I'll never go back.

- 2 t. olive oil (I also use a non-stick pan)
- 1 garlic clove, optional
- 1 T. chopped onion or leek
- 3 fresh mushrooms, chopped
- 1 egg
- 2 egg whites (or use all egg whites)
- 2-3 c. of kale or swiss chard, chopped
- left-over vegetables – asparagus, broccoli, peppers, potatoes
- uncooked tortillas

*Notes*

## *Delicious Healthy Breakfast Burrito Continued*

Brown onions, garlic and mushrooms in 1-2 t. oil. Add chopped kale/swiss chard. Brown lightly. Add vegetables, then turn heat on low. In the meantime, beat eggs in a small bowl with a fork. Add beaten eggs to vegetable mixture. Turn heat on medium and cook until eggs are almost done. Turn on low or off until tortillas are done.

In another non-stick skillet, preheat pan to medium heat. Place tortilla in pan and cook for 30 seconds until slightly golden and puffy. Flip over tortilla and cook until done about 30 sec. Add cooked egg mixture to tortilla and roll up into a burrito. Enjoy!

This recipe makes enough for 2 people. Pair this with a Zhen Qu which is a Yunnan tea and you have an outstanding combination!

Variations:

- Try adding salsa and tomatoes.

- Try adding parmesan cheese (just a wee bit if you want the recipe to stay healthy).

- Try adding black beans.

The possibilities are endless. I find it's the perfect amount of protein and the right kind of carbs. It gets me through until snack time.

*Notes*

## *Easy 40 Clove Garlic Crock Pot Chicken*

When you first see the title of the recipe, you might think, "Yikes! That's a lot of garlic!" But actually the garlic becomes mellow and nutty. A version of this dish was popularized by Julia Child. It's a great dish when having dinner guests because it's quick and easy. All you do is just throw everything in the crock pot and return home to a wonderful aroma, ready to eat. To make preparation easier, buy already peeled garlic (often found at Costco) or drop the garlic cloves in boiling water for a few seconds, drain and allow to cool. The garlic peels will slip off easily with your fingers. Have a loaf of French bread on hand. When the chicken is ready, spread the cooked garlic cloves on bread slices. Use the left-over chicken for Easy Open Faced Chicken and Asparagus Sandwich Melts (page 87).

- 40 cloves of garlic (yes, really!)

*Notes*

## *Easy 40 Clove Garlic Crock Pot Chicken Continued*

- 4 lbs. whole chicken
- 4 celery ribs, sliced
- salt and pepper
- ½ fresh lemon
- 3 sprigs of fresh rosemary
- 3 fresh sage leaves
- 3 sprigs of fresh thyme (I like to use lemon thyme)
- 2 sprigs of Italian parsley
- ¼ c. sherry or chicken broth

Rinse chicken well and pat dry. Inside the chicken cavity, place ½ lemon, 1 sprig of rosemary, 1 sprig of thyme and 1 sage leaf and a few garlic cloves. Slice the celery and place in the bottom of the crock pot. Set chicken on top. Chop up remaining herbs and sprinkle over the chicken. Add salt and pepper to taste. Place the rest of the garlic cloves around the chicken. Pour the sherry over the top. Cook on high for 4-6 hours or on low for 8-10 hours.

Squeeze the roasted garlic out of the skins onto toasted French bread and spread with a knife. Enjoy!

*Notes*

## *Easy Open Faced Chicken and Asparagus Sandwich Melts*

This is a great meal or lunch when you have overnight guests. Start the Easy 40 Clove Garlic Crock Pot Chicken in the morning, serve to guests in the evening, use the left overs for this recipe for lunch or dinner the next day!

- left-over Easy 40 Clove Garlic Crock Pot Chicken (page 83)
- French bread, rolls or any artisian style bread
- butter
- cheese – cheddar or any kind you like
- fresh asparagus spears
- paprika (optional)

Cook asparagus in boiling water or a few minutes in microwave until done. Cut into small pieces. Reheat chicken pieces in microwave a few minutes until hot. Butter bread slices. Spread roasted garlic cloves from left-over chicken recipe onto buttered bread slices. Top with chicken and asparagus. Top with a slice of your favorite cheese. Sprinkle with paprika if desired. Broil in oven for about 2 minutes or until done. Serve hot.

*Notes*

## Käse Spätzle

You can't have schnitzel at our house without making Käse Spätzle. It's a glorified macaroni and cheese. So good! You really need a spätzle maker, you can get them on Amazon.com for about $10.00. I've tried for years using other methods. Some people try and push dough through a colander, but I think the spätzle maker is best.

- 3 c. flour
- 1 t. salt
- 4 eggs, beaten
- water as needed
- 3 T. butter
- 1 t. olive oil
- 2 medium red onions, sliced
- ¾ c. gruyere or swiss cheese, shredded

Carmelize onions by heating 1 T. butter and 1 t. olive oil. Add

*Notes*

## Käse Spätzle Continued

sliced onions. Cook on low for about one hour (while you are making the spätzle), stirring occasionally. Cooking the onions slowly develops the flavor, they become sweet and lightly browned.

While the onions are cooking, grate or shred the cheese, set aside. Butter or spray a 9"x13" pan, set aside.

Fill a large pot with water, add a bit of salt and bring to a boil.

To make the dough, place flour and salt in a mixer or large bowl. Add beaten eggs and mix for several minutes until dough is smooth. It's easier to use an electric mixer or stand mixer. Allow dough to rest for about 10 minutes. Beat again. Add enough water (about ½ c.) to adjust consistency to a thick batter (a little thinner than brownie batter). Place the spätzle maker over the boiling water, reduce heat to simmering. Add about ¼ of the dough into the spätzle maker. Push and pull the hopper back and forth. The noodles will drop to the bottom of the pot and rise to the surface. Allow them to cook another 2-3 minutes and then scoop them out with a slotted spoon. Place in colander and rinse with hot water. Drain and set aside. Do this for the rest of the dough.

When all noodles are done, fry for a bit in butter and then place ½ of them into the 9"x13" pan. Toss with the onions and sprinkle ½ of the cheese on top. Add the rest of noodles and top with more cheese. Cover and bake at 350° for about 15-20 minutes. Uncover and bake at least 15 minutes more. Put broiler on the last few minutes and brown the cheese. Serve hot.

*Notes*

## *Pat's Sliders*

My husband has always made great hamburgers but they were always too big for me. He switched to slider size and now everyone has better portion control, plus the condiments stay on the burger better!

- 1½ lb. hamburger – 80% lean (if you use 90%, the sliders will be dry)
- 1½ T. Ranch dressing mix
- ¼ c. Worchestershire sauce
- ⅓ c. beer
- 1 t. fresh ground pepper
- dinner rolls or slider buns

Mix thoroughly with the hamburger and make into small 3½" patties. Cook on grill until desired doneness. Add cheese if desired.

Toast buns on grill.

Serve sliders with a mixture of condiments such as grilled onions, blue cheese crumbles, diced tomatoes, barbecue sauce, cheese.

Makes about 8-12 sliders.

*Notes*

## *Ginger Scallion Salmon*

This is a quick, easy and delicious meal!

- 6 T. Ginger Scallion Sauce (page 59)
- 2 lbs. salmon filet
- cedar plank (you can find them at a barbeque store or Home Depot, be sure you use non-treated, cooking grade)

Brush the top of salmon filet with Scallion Ginger Sauce. Allow to marinate for at least 30 minutes. Soak cedar plank in water for at least 30 minutes.

Set up grill for direct cooking at moderately high heat.

Place cedar plank on grill for 3-4 minutes to "season" it. Flip the plank over and add the salmon. Cover the grill with lid and cook for 20 minutes or until done when salmon flakes with a fork (internal temperature of salmon should be at least 135°.)

Serves 6

*Notes*

## *Sesame Chicken*

This is another recipe which works well for freezing. Freeze the chicken after you fry it, then just reheat in the oven to crisp it up.

Brine:
- 2 c. buttermilk
- 1 T. salt
- 3 cloves of garlic, minced

Marinade:
- ½ T. sesame oil
- 2 T. soy sauce
- ½ t. cayenne pepper
- 1 garlic clove, minced
- 3 boneless chicken breasts, cut into bite-sized pieces

*Notes*

## *Sesame Chicken Continued*

- 1½ c. flour
- 1 T. cornstarch
- ½ t. baking powder
- ½ t. baking soda
- 1 T. salt

Sauce:

- 1½ c. water
- 2 T. chicken bouillon (or use 2 chicken bouillon cubes)
- ⅓ c. rice vinegar
- ½ c. sugar
- 2 t. sesame oil
- 1½ t. sriracha sauce (use ½ t.-1 t. if you don't like it as spicy)
- 2 garlic cloves minced
- 1 T. sesame seeds
- ¼ c. corn starch
- ½ c. green onions, chopped

In a large bowl, combine, buttermilk, salt, garlic and chicken. Allow to brine overnight or at least 6 hours.

When ready to cook, stir in sesame oil, soy sauce and cayenne to chicken mixture. In a small bowl, combine flour, cornstarch, baking powder and baking soda. Add flour mixture to chicken. Cover and refrigerate while making sauce about

*Notes*

## *Sesame Chicken Continued*

20-30 minutes.

To make the sauce:

Bring 1 c. water, chicken bouillon, vinegar, sugar, sesame oil, sriracha sauce, garlic, sesame seeds to a boil. Place cornstarch in a small bowl. Add ½ c. water. Stir until cornstarch is dissolved and not lumpy. Add cornstarch mixture to sauce. Simmer until the sauce thickens, about 2-3 minutes. Add chopped green onions . Turn heat to low and keep warm until chicken is done.

Heat deep fryer or a large saucepan with oil to medium-high heat. Drain chicken slightly and drop in battered chicken pieces and fry until they turn a deep golden brown. Drain on a paper towel-lined plate.

To serve, place the chicken on a platter and pour the hot sauce over the top and sprinkle with more sesame seeds if desired.

Serves 6.

*Notes*

## Sichuan Chicken Flatbread

This recipe came about because I loved the Sichuan Chicken Flatbread at PF Changs. They took it off the menu so I decided to recreate it. Serve this with Spicy Dragon Sauce (page 63). They make wonderful unique appetizers.

- 3 chicken breasts, raw, chopped finely
- 2 T. sesame oil
- 2 T. Scallion Ginger Sauce (page 59) or use 3 green onions chopped
- salt and pepper to taste
- 1 c. shredded cheddar cheese, Monterey Jack also works well
- 8 Chinese Scallion Pancakes (page 27) or use 8 flour tortillas

Heat sesame oil in a medium skillet, add chopped chicken

*Notes*

## *Sichuan Chicken Flatbread Continued*

and scallion ginger sauce or green onions and cook until chicken is done. Add salt and pepper to taste.

On a cookie sheet, place 2 Chinese scallion pancakes (already fried) side by side (or use tortillas). Cover both with chicken mixture. Sprinkle cheese over the top. Place another pancake/tortilla on top (repeat for the remaining pancakes/tortillas). Bake in oven at 400° for about 10 minutes or until thoroughly heated.

Cut each pancake/tortilla into 4 pieces. Serve with Spicy Dragon Sauce.

Serves 4 or makes 16 appetizers.

*Notes*

## Street Tacos

The marinade below works great for beef, chicken and pork. It tastes best when allowed to marinate overnight.

- 3 T. of Amy's Homemade Taco Seasoning (page 57)
- ⅓ c. lime juice
- ½ c. vegetable/canola oil
- 1 garlic clove, minced
- 1 lb. flank steak or chicken
- Homemade Corn Tortillas (page 35) or flour tortillas
- taco condiments: chopped cilantro, sour cream, shredded cheese, etc.

Combine taco seasoning, lime juice and oil together and pour over 1 pound of flank steak. Spread minced garlic over the top of the steak. Refrigerate for at least 5 hours or overnight.

*Notes*

## *Street Tacos Continued*

Grill and cut diagonally. Serve with tortillas and taco condiments.

You can also cook the meat in the oven. I use a cast iron skillet. I preheat the skillet and oven to 500°. Place half of the meat in the skillet and cook in oven for 2-3 minutes without turning. Then flip meat over and cook until done. Add a pat of butter on top during last 2 minutes of cooking. Cooking time depends on thickness of flank steak and desired doneness. Mine takes about 8-10 minutes total for a medium steak. After removing the steak from the grill or oven, place on a plate and cover with foil for about 10 minutes before cutting. This allows the juices to set in and the meat cuts easier. Slice thinly and serve. You can also freeze the cooked meat for later. Slice into thin strips and freeze. Just warm up before serving.

Also try using the marinade for chicken. Cut up 4 chicken breasts and marinate all day or overnight. Drain marinade and grill until done. Serve over rice, topped with cheese, green onions, avocado, salsa, sour cream, etc. Or serve in tacos or burritos.

Serves 8.

*Notes*

# *Wiener Schnitzel*

Being born in Germany and having lived there many years, I love schnitzel. They are so thin and crisp. In Germany you may often find schnitzel bigger than dinner plates (Elephant Ears)! The secret is to let them sit a few hours before frying them. Of course schnitzel doesn't fall exactly into the ":healthy meal": category, but a nice indulgence every now and then is a must! Serve this with vegetables and Käse Spätzle (page 89) or put it on a nice french roll and eat as a sandwich with mustard and cucumbers. True schnitzel is made with veal, but I make mine with pork tenderloin slices.

- pork tenderloin slices or pork chops
- cracker crumbs, take a few sleeves of crackers and process them in the food processor or crush with a rolling pin
- oregano
- onion powder
- garlic powder

*Notes*

## *Wiener Schnitzel Continued*

- salt
- pepper
- 2-4 eggs, beaten
- flour
- lemon wedges
- oil

Season the meat with salt and pepper. With a sharp knife, split the pork chop almost in two (butterfly it). Open the fold and place it between 2 pieces of parchment paper or freezer bags and pound it as thin as you can get it.

Place crumbs in a wide bowl or on a dinner plate, sprinkle with oregano, onion and garlic powder. Mix together with hands.

In another bowl, beat eggs. Place about ½ c. of flour on a dinner plate. Dip the pounded meat into the flour. Coat both sides. Then dip into the beaten eggs. Last dip both sides into the cracker crumbs, pressing down to absorb the crumbs. Place on a plate. Repeat process with other pieces of pork separating the layers with plastic wrap or parchment paper. Cover entire plate with plastic wrap and chill for at least an hour. That's the secret!

When ready to fry, add about 1 inch of oil to a frying pan. Heat until hot. Fry the schnitzel for about 2 minutes. Flip over and fry other side until done (about 3 minutes total or until golden brown.) Place on a paper towel lined plate. Squeeze a bit of lemon over the schnitzel. Keep warm until ready to serve.

*Notes*

*Desserts*

## *Buttered Rum Sauce Mix*

This is a great mix to have on hand in the freezer. Just use as needed. Serve over Apple Cake (page 119) or make Hot Buttered Rum (recipe below).

- 1 c. unsalted butter, softened
- 1 lb. powdered sugar
- 1 lb. light brown sugar
- 1 qt. of vanilla ice cream, softened
- 2 t. cinnamon
- 1 t. nutmeg
- pinch of cloves
- pinch of salt

In a large mixing bowl, cream together butter and sugars. Add cinnamon, nutmeg, cloves and salt. Stir in softened ice cream. Place mixture in a freezer container with a tight fitting lid. Store in freezer for up to 2 months.

To make a Hot Buttered Rum:

Place 2 heaping tablespoons of Butter Rum Sauce Mix in a glass or mug. Add 1-2 T. of rum. Pour 6 oz. of boiling water over the mix and stir until melted. Sprinkle with a bit of cinnamon.

*Notes*

# *Apple Cake with Buttered Rum Sauce*

This is a quick and easy dessert, especially if you have the Butter Rum Sauce Mix already in the freezer. These make perfect tea desserts when served in tiny glass dishes. Top with rum sauce and sprinkle a little cinnamon over the top.

- ½ c. butter, softened
- 2 c. sugar
- 2 eggs
- 3 c. chopped apples
- 1 c. chopped nuts (optional)
- 2 c. flour
- 1 t. baking powder
- 1 t. baking soda
- 1 T. cinnamon
- ½ t. salt
- ½ t. fresh nutmeg
- Butter Rum Sauce Mix (page 117)

Preheat oven to 325°. Spray a 9"x13" pan with cooking spray.

Cream butter and sugar together. Add eggs. In a small bowl combine: flour, baking powder, baking soda, cinnamon, salt and nutmeg. Add to creamed mixture. Stir in apples and nuts if desired. Spread into pan (batter will be thick) and bake for about 35-40 minutes or until done with a toothpick. When cool, cut into 1 inch squares and place into a tiny glass serving dish or on individual plates. Top with a dollop of Butter Rum Sauce Mix mixed with 1 t. rum if desired.

You can also pop the individual pieces in the microwave for a few seconds to melt the sauce a bit before devouring.

*Notes*

# Caramel Choc Bars

This is an adapted version of my Chocolate Oatmeals Delights/Choc Bars. I loved the original recipe, but the homemade caramel layer in this one makes this my new favorite!

- 2 c. unsalted butter
- 3 c. brown sugar
- 2 eggs
- 2½ c. flour
- 1 t. salt
- 1 t. baking soda
- 3 c. oatmeal
- 12 oz. semisweet chocolate chips
- 1 can sweetened condensed milk

*Notes*

## *Caramel Choc Bars Continued*

- 2 T. butter
- 1 c. pecans, chopped
- 1 t. vanilla

Cream together 1 c. butter, 2 c. brown sugar and eggs. Sift together flour, salt and baking soda. Add to creamed mixture. Stir in oatmeal. Press ¾ of mixture into a 9"x13" pan. (Reserve the remaining ¼ mixture.)

Melt together chocolate chips, sweetened condensed milk and 2 T. butter. You can do this on a stove on low heat or in the microwave, 30 seconds at a time, stirring well before microwaving again.

Pour chocolate mixture over oatmeal mixture.

In a saucepan, combine 1 c. unsalted butter and 1 c. brown sugar. Bring to a boil and boil for 2 minutes stirring constantly. The mixture will get bubbly and foamy. Turn off heat and add vanilla. Immediately pour over chocolate layer. Sprinkle chopped pecans over caramel layer.

Crumble/chunk the reserved oatmeal mixture on the top of the chocolate mixture. Bake at 350° for 20 minutes. Do not over-bake. The top oatmeal chunky layer will be almost done.

My favorite way to make these is to line a pan with parchment paper. Then spray with cooking spray. Continue following recipe instructions. Let sit overnight. Take a knife and run along the edge. Flip pan over to release bars. Peel off

*Notes*

## *Caramel Choc Bars Continued*

paper and flip over so that bars are right side up. Cut into bars.

This recipe makes about 40 bars.

For best results, let set overnight before cutting or at least 6 hours, otherwise they will be too gooey when you try and cut them.

*Notes*

## *Easy Raspberry Lime Tarts*

I just love this recipe. It's based on my lemon curd recipe and is so easy, yet looks elegant. I prefer the Pepperidge Farm Mini Tart Shells, but I can't always find them. They are in the freezer section. If I can't find them I use the phyllo cups as they work very well too.

- ½ c. butter
- 1 c. sugar
- ½ c. lime juice
- 3 eggs
- 2 pkg. mini tarts or phyllo cups
- fresh raspberries, rinsed and drained
- zest of 2 limes

Melt butter in microwave for about 1 minute. Beat eggs in a glass bowl with an electric mixer until frothy. Mix in

*Notes*

## *Easy Raspberry Lime Tarts Continued*

butter, sugar, and lime juice. Microwave on high for 3 minutes. Beat mixture again until smooth. Microwave again for another 3 minutes. Beat mixture again until smooth. Refrigerate until set. Lime curd will keep up to 2 weeks in refrigerator.

To make tarts:

Fill tart or phyllo cup with about 1 t. of lime curd. Top with an upside down raspberry and sprinkle lime zest over the top. Serve immediately or place in the refrigerator until ready to serve.

Makes about 30 tarts.

*Notes*

## *Easy Sea Salt Toffee Candy*

My good friend, Amy Nelson, gave me this recipe. She calls it, "Crack". I adapted it a bit. Be forewarned, it is very addicting. There's just something special about the sweetness of the chocolate and caramel and the saltiness of the saltines. It is absolutely wonderful, and so easy to make. You can't just eat one!

- 4 oz. saltine crackers (one sleeve)
- 1 c. butter
- 1 c. brown sugar
- 1 t. vanilla
- 1 12 oz. pkg of toffee bits
- 2 c. semisweet chocolate chips
- ¾ c. chopped pecans, or try walnuts, pecans or almonds
- sea salt

# Notes

## *Easy Sea Salt Toffee Candy Continued*

Preheat oven to 400°. Line a cookie sheet (with sides) or jelly roll pan with aluminum foil and spray with vegetable spray. Arrange saltines in a single layer on the cookie sheet.

In a saucepan, combine the sugar and butter. Bring to a boil and boil for exactly 3 minutes. Remove from heat and stir in vanilla. Immediately pour caramel mixture over the saltines and spread to cover crackers. Don't worry if it doesn't cover it completely. Sprinkle toffee bits over the caramel. Bake at 400° for 5 minutes. Remove from oven and sprinkle chocolate chips over the top. Let sit for a few minutes and then spread melted chocolate. Top with chopped nuts and sprinkle sea salt. Cool completely and break into pieces.

Save any crumbs (freeze in a plastic bag) to use for ice cream topping.

*Notes*

# Jamaican Banana Cheesecake

This is a creamy cheesecake. It looks like a lot of work, but actually goes very fast. It will not be set when it comes out of the oven. Be sure and let it set up overnight or make it early in the morning to serve after dinner. You can make it in a 9"x13" pan or a spring form pan.

Crust:
- ¼ c. butter
- ¼ c. brown sugar
- 1½ c. vanilla wafer, crushed
- 1 T. fresh lime rind

Filling:
- 1½ lb. cream cheese, softened
- 2 mashed bananas
- 1 c. sugar

*Notes*

## *Jamaican Banana Cheesecake Continued*

- 1½ T. cornstarch
- 1½ T. vanilla
- 1 T. rum
- 1 T. lime juice
- 4 eggs
- dash of salt

Topping:
- 2 c. sour cream
- ¼ c. sugar
- 1 T. vanilla

Sauce:
- ¼ c. butter
- 2 T. rum
- ½ c. brown sugar
- 2 T. lime juice
- ½ c. coconut
- 1 c. pecans
- lime slices for garnish

In a food processor, crush vanilla wafers until very fine. In a small bowl, add crushed vanilla wafers, lime rind, brown sugar and melted butter. Stir until crumbs are well moistened. If it seems a bit too dry, add a little more melted butter. Place in a nonstick 9 inch or larger spring form pan, or in a 9"x13" pan sprayed with cooking spray. Place in freezer until filling is ready.

*Notes*

## *Jamaican Banana Cheesecake Continued*

In a large mixing bowl or mixer, add softened cream cheese, sugar and bananas. Cream together until cream cheese is smooth and lumps are gone. Mix in cornstarch, vanilla, rum, lime juice, dash of salt and eggs. Beat until smooth.

Pour filling into prepared a 9 inch spring form or 9"x13" pan. Bake at 350° for 30-45 minutes. The edges will be set, the middle will jiggle slightly. Have topping ready and when cheesecake is done, lightly dollop sour cream mixture around the edges of the cheesecake. Carefully spread topping across the middle. If you dollop directly on the middle, the cake will fall, so start with going around the edges and then across to cover the middle. If cheesecake falls, don't worry. You can always make a bit more topping to cover it after it's done. Return cheesecake to oven and bake for 5 more minutes at 450°.

Cheesecake will not be set in the middle. Cool on a wire rack for at least 30 minutes and then place in refrigerator. Allow to set up over night.

Before serving, make Jamaican sauce by combining: butter, rum, brown sugar, lime juice, coconut and pecans. Cook on stove top until butter is melted and mixture starts to boil. Cool for a few minutes and then pour over cheesecake. Allow to set up for 20 minutes and then cut and serve. You can also put the sauce in a gravy dish or small pitcher and pour over the individual slices of cheesecake when you serve it. Garnish with lime slices.

*Notes*

# *Oodles (Oatmeal Snickerdoodles)*

My kids absolutely adore these!

- 1 ½ c. flour
- 1 ½ c. oatmeal (not instant)
- 2 t. cream of tartar
- 1 t. baking soda
- ¼ t. salt
- 1 T. cinnamon
- ½ c. (1 stick) of unsalted butter
- ½ c. butter-flavored Crisco
- ¾ c. sugar
- ¾ c. brown sugar
- 2 eggs
- 1 t. vanilla

*Notes*

# *Oodles (Oatmeal Snickerdoodles) Continued*

- Extra cinnamon and sugar to coat the balls

Preheat oven to 400°. Line baking sheets with parchment paper.

Grind oatmeal in the food processor until fine.

In a medium bowl, mix together flour, ground oatmeal, cream of tartar, baking soda, salt and cinnamon. Set aside.

Cream sugars, shortening and unsalted butter until light and fluffy (about 2 minutes) with mixer. Scrape sides of bowl often. Add eggs and vanilla. Beat well. Add dry ingredients.

In a small bowl, combine about ¼ c. sugar and 1-2 T. cinnamon. Use a small ice-cream scoop to form balls of dough. My scoop is 1½ inches in diameter. You can also use the "Perfect Pot of Tea" measuring spoon if you have one. It's the same size. Roll balls in cinnamon/sugar mixture and place on prepared baking pans about 2 inches apart. Bake about 8-10 minutes. After removing cookies from oven, leave on pans for about 5 minutes before moving them to wire racks.

Store in an airtight container. If you add a slice of bread to the container, the cookies will stay soft.

Makes about 3 dozen large cookies.

*Notes*

# Orange Walnut Scones

You can use store bought orange peel, but the fresh peel really makes a difference.

- 3 c. self-rising flour
- ¼ c. brown sugar
- ¼ c. sugar
- 1 T. freshly grated orange peel
- 1 c. finely chopped walnuts
- 1 stick unsalted butter
- ¾ c. buttermilk (sometimes you may need to add a bit more)
- ¼ c. orange juice

Glaze:
- 1 c. powdered sugar
- 1 T. freshly grated orange peel

*Notes*

## *Orange Walnut Scones Continued*

- orange juice (about ¼ c.)

Preheat oven to 400°.

Combine flour, sugars, orange peel, walnuts in a large bowl. Cut in butter with a pastry blender or fork until mixture is course and crumbly. Mix ¼ c. orange juice and ¾ c. buttermilk together. Add just enough buttermilk mixture to make a soft dough. If you need a bit more add a little more buttermilk. Scoop out about ⅓ of the dough and form a small disc about 8 inches in diameter and about ½ inch thick (the width of your pinky finger). Cut into 8 pie-shaped pieces. Do this for the remaining dough. Place on a cookie sheet lined with parchment paper and bake about 8-10 minutes until done (depending on your oven). To make glaze: combine powdered sugar and orange peel. Add enough orange juice to make desired consistency. Dip scones into glaze and allow to set, or you can drizzle glaze over the scoens. Enjoy!

These can be frozen and reheated in foil.

Makes about 15 scones.

*Notes*

## *Peppermint Brittle*

This recipe is in our second cookbook, "A Little of This and a Little of That", however I have made a few changes over the years, mainly the length of time you bake it. In this version I have also doubled the recipe and have used a cookie sheet instead of a 9"x13" pan.

- 3 c. flour
- 1 t. baking soda
- ½ t. salt
- 1½ c. unsalted butter-melted and cooled slightly
- 1 c. sugar
- ⅔ c. brown sugar
- 2 t. vanilla
- 3 c. white chocolate chips
- 1-3 t. vegetable oil to thin white chocolate topping
- 2 c. small candy canes crushed (put them in a plastic bag and crush them with a hammer)

*Notes*

## *Peppermint Brittle Continued*

Preheat oven to 350°. Line a baking sheet with parchment paper. Spray parchment sheet and corners with cooking spray.

In a medium mixing bowl, stir together flour, baking soda and salt. In a large bowl stir in melted butter, both sugars and vanilla until smooth. Stir in flour mixture until just blended. Stir in 2 c. white chocolate chips and 1 c. crushed candy canes. Press dough onto parchment paper on cookie sheet.

Bake for about 15-20 minutes until dough looks set and golden. Be careful not to bake too long otherwise they will be hard to cut.

Before brittle is totally cool, take a knife and score the brittle into pieces. Finish cooling. When cool, melt 1 c. white chocolate chips in microwave 30 seconds at a time until melted. Drizzle over brittle. Sprinkle remaining peppermint pieces over glaze and allow to set. If you need to thin the chocolate glaze, add a few drops of vegetable oil to chocolate.

This recipe makes about 55 pieces. I like to cut mine in squares and then diagonally into triangle pieces.

Store in an airtight container. Enjoy! Caution! You can't just eat one!

*Notes*

*Drinks*

# *Ginger Syrup*

I love to add a few tablespoons of this syrup to a nice iced Ceylon tea or use it in Pat's Ecotinis (page 157). Fresh ginger root is a must!

- 2½ c. water
- 1 c. sugar (I like to use baker's sugar as it dissolves quickly)
- 2 oz. piece of fresh ginger root, peeled and cut into cubes

Process peeled ginger in the food processor. Bring water, sugar, and chopped ginger to a boil. Simmer for 10 minutes; let cool. Strain and place into plastic or glass container. I save unique jars and bottles and use them for my syrup. Ginger Syrup will keep up to 2-3 weeks in the refrigerator.

*Notes*

## *Pat's Ecotinis*

We had these on our Disney cruise to the Mexican Riveria. My husband, Pat, learned how to make them from Jesús, the bartender. They are made with Veev which is an Açaí Berry spirit.

- 2 oz. Veev Açaí Spirit
- 1 oz. triple sec.
- 2 oz. fresh lime juice.
- 1 oz. Ginger Syrup (page 155)
- 1 oz. agave nectar or agave syrup
- ice

Add all ingredients to a cocktail shaker. Shake, pour and enjoy!

*Notes*

## *Peach Bowle*

I first had Bowle in college while studying in Munich, Germany. There are many versions of it. Strawberry Bowle is also very popular, but peach is my favorite! Be sure you use a good quality Riesling and sparkling wine or you may get a bad hangover!

- 8 fresh ripe peaches (or buy fresh frozen peaches), chopped
- 3 T. sugar (I like to use baker's sugar for this as it's finer but regular will do)
- 1 lemon
- 1 bottle of sparkling wine or champagne
- 2 bottles of Riesling
- ½ c. cognac

Slice peaches and chop into small bite-sized chunks. Place in a punch bowl or large bowl. Sprinkle sugar over peaches and stir. Add cognac and 1 bottle of Riesling. Chill for at least 2 hours. Before serving add the other bottle of Riesling and the bottle of sparkling white wine or champagne. Stir gently and serve in a glass or punch cup with cocktail picks so guests can eat the peaches.

*Notes*

# *Index*

| | |
|---|---|
| Amarula Brown Sugar Pecan Brie | 15 |
| Amy's Homemade Taco Seasoning | 57 |
| Amy's Suiza Con Pollo Enchiladas | 67 |
| Apple Cake with Buttered Rum Sauce | 119 |
| Asparagus and Ham Roll Ups | 19 |
| Buttered Rum Sauce Mix | 117 |
| Cajun French Bread | 21 |
| Cantaloup Caprese Salad | 71 |
| Caprese Salad | 73 |
| Caramel Choc Bars | 121 |
| Chicken Sichuan Egg Rolls | 23 |
| Chinese Scallion Pancakes | 27 |
| Chipotle Salsa | 31 |
| Cilantro Pork Crock Pot | 77 |
| Delicious Healthy Breakfast Burrito | 79 |
| Easy 40 Clove Garlic Crock Pot Chicken | 83 |
| Easy Open Faced Chicken and Asparagus Sandwich Melts | 87 |
| Easy Raspberry Lime Tarts | 127 |
| Easy Sea Salt Toffee Candy | 131 |
| Fresh Tomato and Mozzarella Kabobs | 33 |
| Ginger Scallion Salmon | 95 |
| Ginger Scallion Sauce | 59 |
| Ginger Syrup | 155 |
| Homemade Corn Tortillas | 35 |

## Index Continued

| | |
|---|---|
| Homemade Salami Made with Lapsang Souchong Tea | 37 |
| Jamaican Banana Cheesecake | 135 |
| Käse Spätzle | 89 |
| Oodles (Oatmeal Snickerdoodles) | 141 |
| Orange Walnut Scones | 145 |
| Pat's Ecotinis | 157 |
| Pat's Sliders | 93 |
| Peach Bowle | 159 |
| Peppermint Brittle | 149 |
| Rosemary Garlic Parmesan Pinwheels | 41 |
| Savory Ham and Cheddar Scones | 45 |
| Sesame Chicken | 97 |
| Sichuan Chicken Flatbread | 103 |
| Spicy Dragon Sauce | 63 |
| Street Tacos | 107 |
| Sundried Tomato Dip | 49 |
| Tomatillo Green Salsa | 51 |
| Wiener Schnitzel | 111 |

## *About the Author*

Amy Lawrence is an example for women who have had many successful careers in life, including teacher and business owner. With a master's degree in Special Education, she taught for 11 years. In 2003 she decided to pursue her passion and opened her tea room, An Afternoon to Remember. It won many awards including Best Small Tea Room in the U.S. in 2006, KCRA's A-List in 2007, 2008 and 2009, and Sacramento Magazine's Best Tea Room in 2008. In 2009, Amy closed her tea room in order to devote herself full-time to her family and other companies: Afternoon to Remember Fine Tea and Gifts and ATR Publishing.

Amy has published eleven books and sold more than 14,000 of them. She currently lives in Seattle where you can find her selling fine teas and cookbooks at local farmer's markets as well as online at www.afternoontoremember.com.

# Also from ATR Publishing

*Creating an Afternoon to Remember*

*A Little of This and a Little of That*

*Making It Your Own Afternoon to Remember*

*Tea Time Tidbits and Treats*

*Drop by for Tea*

*Master Tea Room Recipes*

*Order them online at http://www.afternoontoremember.com/*

www.ingramcontent.com/pod-product-compliance
Lightning Source LLC
Chambersburg PA
CBHW042311150426
43199CB00001B/1